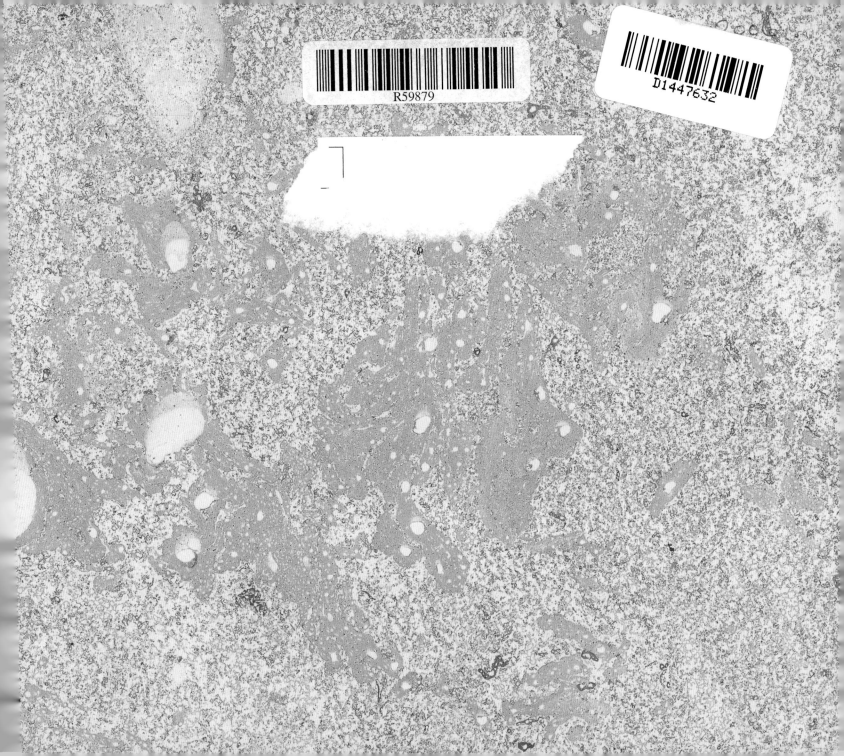

Graham Clarke's

KENT

914.223
CLA

Graham Clarke's

KENT

GRAHAM CLARKE

THIRD MILLENNIUM PUBLISHING

AYLESFORD

The Bridge and St Peter & St Paul

One of the oldest occupied sites in all England and justly popular with visitors including Hengist & Horsa who defeated the locals in A.D. 500 something. To even things up Alfred the Great beat the Danes in A.D. 893 So that's alright.

First published 2000 by Graham Clarke Limited &
Third Millennium Publishing Limited
Shawlands Court, Lingfield, Surrey RH7 6BL

Supported by Kent County Council

ISBN 0 9536969 3 6

A catalogue record of this book is available from the
British Library

Printed in Italy by Valente on Fedrigoni Arcoprint

INTRODUCTION

Sometime in the 1790s an industrious person by the name of James Clarke arrived in Gravesend and rented land around the riverside town from the Lords Darnley of Cobham Hall. He planted, cultivated, mowed and pruned, called it Clarke's Nursery Garden and opened to the public. They came smoke-pickled down from London by boat and later by steam train to enjoy the walks and conservatories, take in the fresh air and take home saffron or asparagus. Visitors could also purchase exotic plants from across the globe propagated from specimens brought home by returning sailors. The enterprise became famous and very much responsible for making Gravesend a popular resort for half a century.

Although he didn't realise it at the time James Clarke was my great great great great grandfather. His sons Charles and England (the latter born on the day the Battle of Trafalgar was won) in due course took over, though sadly missed the quite legitimate opportunity to rename the establishment 'The Garden of England'.

Charles Dickens was a regular visitor to Gravesend and wrote of the Garden in his diaries. When he purchased his house Gad's Hill in nearby Higham naturally he asked Clarke's to lay out his own gardens for him. By this time Arthur George, son of Charles, was in charge. So pleased was Mr Dickens with the work it is said that he gave the small boy helping his father a shilling. What the little rascal (my great grandfather) frittered it away on family legend does not relate.

Opposite Gad's Hill the street runs down to a pleasant Victorian pub 'The Gardeners Arms'. The sign hanging outside portrays a jolly looking chap proudly displaying the fruits (and vegetables) of his labours. He has some Clarkish looks about him and, given that Arthur George Clarke was the best known man of his profession in the district in mid-Victorian times, I suggest that this person is none other than my great great grandfather, and if it isn't it certainly should be say I.

That was my ancestor's contribution to the Garden of England and this collection of watercolours is mine. It will be noticed that in my selection of subjects I have tended towards castles, churches, cottages and the seashore, my favourite subjects. Thereby many a famous and splendid building or popular tourist attraction does not appear, something that could be remedied if there should be a Volume II. It would, however, take several dozen volumes to do the job completely. Not least because we have more buildings of historic and architectural interest than any other county except London and ours are on average a great deal older.

My captions to the watercolours offer little in the way of useful information. For those inclined to learn more I

recommend *A History of Kent* by
F. W. Jessup, *Kent* by Nigel Nicolson and
The Kent Village Book by Alan Bignell, a
treasure house of events and anecdotes
and particularly useful to me in
preparing this work. I also acknowledge
with gratitude the support of Kent
County Council, enthusiastic patrons of
the arts that they are.

I trust that this book goes some way to
illustrate that Kent is still beautiful and
urge all who agree with me to take the
very greatest care of this our wonderful
Garden of England.

Graham Clarke

Boughton Monchelsea
January 2000

APPLEDORE

Horne's Place Oratory

The Horne's arrived in 1366, but in 1380 the French attacked Appledore and burnt down the church and village. Horne's Place lies a mile away and thus escaped, maybe they built this nice little chapel in gratitude?

BARMING

St. Margarets

Places with names ending in 'ing' are Jutish in origin, Barming, Yalding, Malling etc. Long before the Jutes arrived the Romans liked it too and kindly left "remains" close by this fine church.

BILSINGTON

The Church

This tiny place has far more than its 'fair share' of history. Not least that the owner of the Manor was required to carry the last dish of the second course to the King's table and to present him with three maple cups at a Coronation.

BOUGHTON MONCHELSEA

St. Peters lychgate

Built in the 15th Century and we like to think one of the finest in the country. The seats along each side are much appreciated by walkers of the Greensand Way.

BOXLEY

St. Marys & All Saints

Boxley was a major provider of that vital requirement of the Kentish Broadcloth Industry, Fullers Earth, the degreasing agent.

BRENCHLEY

All Saints Church

With its ancient Yew trees kept trimmed by men paid a Quart of beer per tree. Is that a quart each man or between the lot?

It's Important.

BRENCHLEY

The Halfway House

It's close to Brenchley
but not obviously
'Halfway' to anywhere
else. It looks a nice
enough pub though.

BRENZETT

St. Eanswith's

She was the granddaughter of
King Ethelbert and founded
in 630 of the first nunnery
in England at Folkestone.
A carpenter building the nunnery
cut a length of timber too short
She lengthened it "by prayer",
a decent customer.

BROADSTAIRS

The Harbourmasters

From this very place at the impressionable age of six we set sail early one morning and I caught my first fish. Never to be forgotten.

12 ft. 6 ins. (Nearly)

BROADSTAIRS

The Jetty

How we love this place, the most perfect little seaside town in the South East. Charles Dickens loved it too and stayed in our Honeymoon hotel when working on his books. He left just before we arrived.

CRANBROOK

The Smock Mill

This famous mill was built in 1814. long before that Cranbrook was for 300 years one of the largest and wealthiest towns in Kent, centre of Clothmaking and the woollen Industry.

DUNGENESS

Fishermans Railway

To transport catch andgear across the vast expanse of shingle, Kent's very own desert. Strange plants notrees and a vast assortment of migrating birds also excellent little fish shops adjacent to the fishermens homes.

DUNGENESS

Open Beach

These must be the largest
boats in England to be
hauled up on a beach.
'Dover Soles' and 'Whitstable
Oysters' you have heard of
but did you know that in
California our Common
Crab is known as a
"Dungeness?"   [true]

DUNGENESS

Prospect Cottage

Now a shrine to a famous film
maker. This is as I remember
the cottage 25 years ago.
"Built as a cage for my canary
who sang all her life" the
old man told me.

EAST SUTTON

The church

One of my favourite Kent
churches which can be
enjoyed by all those pre-
pared to walk the long
distance Greensand Way.

EASTLING

Tong House

An old farmstead amid the
rolling and fruitful North
Downs south west of
Faversham.

EDENBRIDGE

The King & Queen

The pub and a row of old shops. Even with the main road slap through the middle it's still a pleasant place. Kent's far western outpost.

EYNSFORD

Old Cottages

With the sparkling river Darent opposite, the Plough just next door, a Roman Villa up the road and a Norman Castle down the road who could ask for more?

EYNSFORD

St. Martin's Church

Around the clock is inscribed
"Grow old along with me the
best is yet to be"
> Robert Browning

To which I suppose the obvious
reply must be :-
"Should I grow old with thee,
then that's O.K. by me".

FAIRFIELD

The Church

The Church and not much else
not even a hamlet.
Just lots of sheep lots of water
and more sheep. None the-
less it's a wonderful place.

FAVERSHAM

The Brewery

Shepherd Neame's famous
brewery the oldest in all
England and still brewing
good stuff, also lending
a pleasant aroma to its
fine old town — free.

FAVERSHAM

The Creek

A beautifully preserved old
market town and ancient
port still at work.

FOLKESTONE

the Harbour

Shellfish gluttons look no further, stroll along the quayside and take your pick.

FRESH CRAB
SANDWICHES

GRAFTY GREEN

Henry Town

Of Grafty Green in the parish of Boughton Malherbe, in this book because I told him he would be.

GRAVESEND

Floating Dock.

lots of lovely boaty business goes on here as it has for several hundred years.

HALLING

Baptist Church

Halling was for half a century practically the cement producing capital of all England.
This pretty little building is appropriately made of corrugated iron .

49

HARTY FERRY

Across the Swale

Sadly there is no longer a ferry here. To go the long way round by road is well worth while just to visit the little church, the most remote in the county.

HEADCORN

The Churchyard

Why this angel should look quite so distressed I don't know, this is such a lovely place. Beyond the church is Headcorn Manor one of the splendid Hall Houses of the Weald.

HERNE BAY

the Promenade

Old fashioned and not much of a 'bay' as the coast is more or less dead straight, but it's been the venue for a million Londoners happy holidays.

HERNHILL

the Manor House

At the South East corner of the perfect village green. In the churchyard lies Mad Thom the self proclaimed messiah who in 1838 came off second best in the Battle of Bossenden Wood.

HEVER

Cottages

Timber frame, tiles and plasterwork beneath a thatched roof, a humble cottage in it's nice little garden. Just around the corner from the rather more splendid Castle.

HOLLINGBOURNE

Cotts by the A20

A row of little cottages hanging onto each other by the busy main road. Almost as memorable from childhood travels as the lovely Castle a mile further on.

HORSMONDEN

St. Margarets

An important ironworking
centre was Horsmonden,
making Guns and Cannon
to fight for King & Country
and perhaps just a few
to smuggle abroad?

HYTHE

The Beach
A thriving fishing community.
Beyond, the Martello towers
built as a deterrent to Napoleon,
they must have worked because
he never came.

IDEN GREEN

Frane Farm

The cherry orchards have long gone but how we used to enjoy calling in on our way down to Rye to buy from the pickers camped beneath the trees.

EARLY RIVERS 2/6

LAMBERHURST

Two Geese

A typical tile-hung farm-house of the rolling High Weald, orchards, hops and woodland.

LAMBERHURST

Old Cottages & Oast

Go a few more yards and you will find yourself in Sussex. But Lamberhurst chose to live in Kent (as there was a better price for hops) very sensible too.

LEEDS

St. Nicholas

The second largest church tower in Kent they say. They must mean girth rather than height of course. "Short, Fat & Lovely" is St. Nicholas.

LEEDS CASTLE

The Gloriette

There has been a Castle
here for a thousand years
a favourite home for
Kings & Queens over the
centuries, and now for
all of us to enjoy.

LEEDS CASTLE

The Gatehouse

Pretend you're a knight or a
prince, a lady in waiting or
even a Queen and cross
this ancient stone bridge.
Plenty of real ones have
and you can too.

LENHAM

the Dog & Bear

An old coaching inn on the famous village square. Justly proud of its' Royal Patronage.

LOOSE

The stream

This waterway has provided power for fulling mills and paper mills and clean waters for watercress since Saxon times, and continues its' importance as an excellent place for children to get their feet soaking wet.

LOWER HALSTOW

St. Margaret of Antioch

Rarely are churchyard walls and salty waters such close neighbours.

MAIDSTONE

Ye Olde Thirsty Pig

This ancient building has changed its name several times since we have been around so who know how many changes since it was built?

Knight rides street keeps its marvellously evocative name on a more permanent basis.

←

OARE

<u>The Three Mariners</u>

A watery village of creeks
and boats.
One mariner looks as though
he's getting thirsty waiting
for the other two.

→

OLD ROMNEY

<u>St. Clements</u>

Its hard to believe but Old
Romney was one of the
original Cinque Ports.
Nowadays St. Clements sits
peacefully guarding the
sheep several miles from
the sea.

PENSHURST
the Gatehouse

Through the arch, turn left and you're in one of the finest gardens in Kent.

QUEENBOROUGH
the Creek

"Miserable, Dirty, Decayed, Poor, Pitiful ~~Fishing~~ Town"
(Daniel Defoe)
1670

I like it and so did Nelson & Lady Hamilton.
G.C.

RAINHAM

Rainham Creek

Beneath these tranquil waters lie huge Roman Potteries the largest in the land. Their products were shattered and scattered for the delight of our archaeologists - how kind.

RAMSGATE

Marina Esplanade

Take a pleasant stroll towards the East Cliff and call in at the Marina Restaurant on your way back.

RAMSGATE

The Shipwrights Arms

Not a lot of Shipbuilding here now but Ramsgate is still a fine town with every right to be proud of itself. Theres nothing to out shine it on the opposite side of the Channel.

Ramsgate Mean Time is 5 Mins. 41 Secs. faster than this Clock

MARITIME MUSEUM

ROCHESTER

Castle & Cathedral

Kents' second city where Watling Street crosses the Medway. The great stone Keep of the Castle keeps close company with the beautiful Cathedral.

RINGWOULD

Front Street Back Street

By the side of the Dover Road to Deal with a most unusual brick and flint church. These two streets are most conveniently named.

ROLVENDEN

The Windmill

The best surviving example of a post mill in the County. Restored in 1956 as a memorial to a young man who "lived his short life within sight of it."

ST. MARY IN THE MARSH

St. Marys

A fine church with its sturdy Norman tower, remote amongst the silent mysteries of the Romney Marsh.

ST. MARY'S HOO

The Church

Wild and windy is the Hoo Peninsula 'Kents Arctic' at the worst of times. But this little corner is cosy enough a nice old church, a pond, a few farms and their cottages.

SALTWOOD

Cottage by the Castle

A long time ago those four
zealous knights planned
the murder of Thomas à
Becket in this Castle.
In 1954 another knight bought
it, Sir Kenneth Clark (my
kind patron) and considered
it the most beautiful place
in the world.

SANDWICH

The Barbican Gate

"An old decayed miserable
town"... (Daniel Defoe)

"As villanous a hole as
one could wish to see"
(William Cobbett)

"A most precious jewel
in the Kentish Crown"
(Graham Clarke)

SARRE

The Windmill

This Smock Mill built in 1820 became a 'Smoke Mill' as you might say 100 yrs late when it became the first Kent mill to be powered by steam. Now restored the sweeps turn again.

SHEERNESS

The Sea Wall

This impressive sea defence and esplanade gazes across the murky waters of the Thames Estuary.

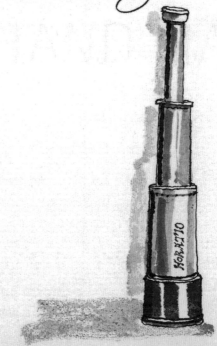

SHOREHAM

Holly Place

A lovely huddle of timber framed domestic buildings in Samuel Palmer's Shoreham. A village & pilgrimage for Wendy & I in our younger days.

SMARDEN

The Churchyard

This pretty village is pleased to inform us that it has won the Best Kept Village award on numerous occasions, and quite right too.

SNODLAND

Battle of the Medway

Round about here in A.D. 43 our man Caratacus leading the British Tribes was defeated by a Roman Army. They had cheated by swimming the Medway wearing suits of armour.

STONE IN OXNEY

Isle of Oxen

A Stone church and a fine timbered house with a spectacular view across the Romney Marsh all the way down to Dungeness.

STROOD

Temple Marsh

Looking South from Strood up the Medway. Boats barges and the occasional paddle steamer all for our leisure and pleasure. You will find working boats just a mile down stream.

TESTON

Alfred Reader

The famous Cricket & Hockey Ball factory. The workers formed their own Trade Union, the smallest in the land the Teston Independant Society of Cricket Ball Makers. The 10 M.P.H. sign is to limit the speed of vehicles not to prevent fast bowling.

THREE CHIMNEYS

Oast Houses

French prisoners residing in Sissinghurst Castle during the Napoleonic wars (if they behaved themselves) were allowed to walk as far as 'Les Trois Chemins' which gave it's name to the cosy pub. Curious because four roads meet here.

TONBRIDGE

the Castle

The gatehouse to the 13th Century castle, it's fearsome appearance does not seem to have spoiled the little girls bat and ball or put the workmen off their lunch.

WALMER

The Castle

Henry VIIII built these 'crouching style' castles, in Kent they gave cover to the five ships that beat the Armada. Warden of the Cinque Ports Duke of Wellington died here. Whether he had his famous boots on at the time is not recorded.

WESTWELL

The Beacon

A spot on the hills just above this quiet farm was once the very heart of Kentish Communications the Westwell Beacon Very handy if you were expecting an Armada, not too good if the weather was misty.

WHITSTABLE

Pearsons

Oysters they say have been cultivated in these salty waters for 2000 years. Now a luxury, in times gone by they were 'poor mans food'.

Actually I like whelks and they're still underrated.

'He's quite right.'

WHITSTABLE

The New Harbour

Fine new buildings to accomodate the famous Whitstable fishermen and their steamy whelk boiling activities. Excellent fish shops too.

WHITSTABLE OYSTER YAWL 1890

WILLESBOROUGH

the windmill

A fine restored windmill
near Ashford, they are
both useful and beautiful
with limitless resources of
power. Bring them back we
say.

WOODCHURCH

Marble Paths

with footpaths of Bethersden
'marble', not a real marble
but a very useful stone
which has enabled transport
across Kents boggier regions
for hundreds of years.

YALDING

Town Bridge

Where the Mid Kent rivers
the Beult and Teise meet
old Father Medway. A
very pleasant village if
a 'bit watery' from time
to time.

YALDING

Randall Cottages

There are not very many
thatched buildings in
Kent but here's an interesting
exception. Just down the
road a sign over a cottage
door announces 'hats by
Retail'.

BOUGHTON MONCHELSEA

The Gardeners Arms

An old cottage in our back garden that now forms the entrance to my studio. Here for very many years lived old Myrt a professional gardener. We named it The Gardeners Arms in her memory.

MYRTS GARDEN

MYRTLE MEDHURST
1894 : 1984

INDEX

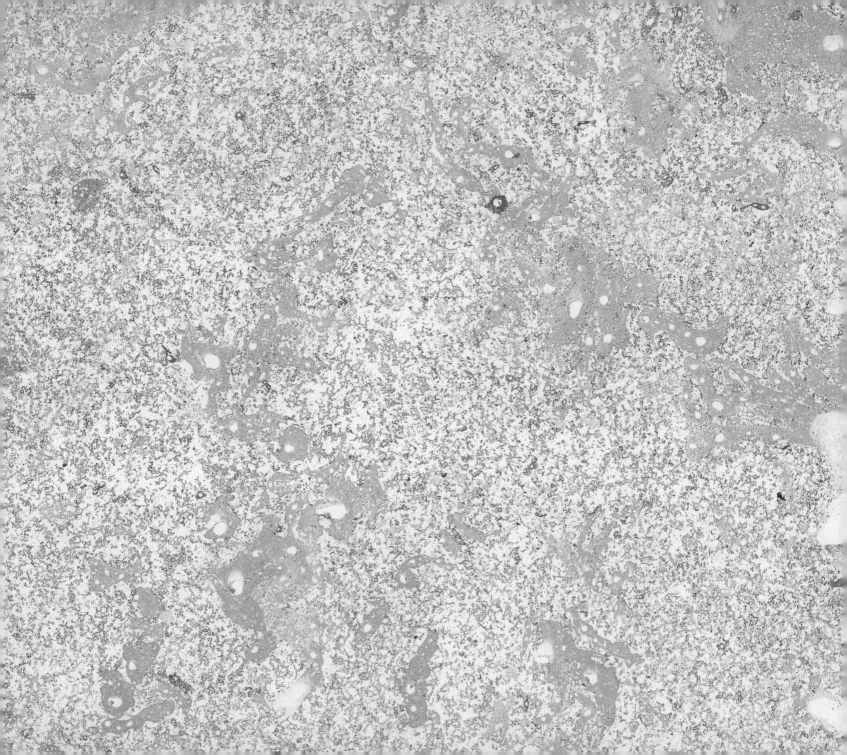